The Gift of Peace

Thoughts For A Peaceful World

D0995126

Brahma Kumaris

The Gift of Peace
Thoughts For A Peaceful World

Author Enrique Simó

Reprint January 2007

First Edition August 2002
First Published in English
ISBN No. 1-886872-24-4

Published by Brahma Kumaris Information Services Ltd., in
association with Brahma Kumaris World Spiritual University (UK)
Registered Charity No. 269971.
Global Co-operation House, 65 Pound Lane, London NW10 2HH, UK

Designed by Infograf, London, UK

www. bkpublications.com
email: enquiries@bkpublications.com

www.bkwsu.org

Preface

While flying to New York three weeks after the 11th September 2001 tragedies, a long-serving student and teacher of the Brahma Kumaris World Spiritual University (BKWSU) realised he had two alternatives. One was to be worried and create thoughts of fear and insecurity. The other was to create thoughts of peace that would help him feel calm and create a good atmosphere all around.

At that moment, he decided to write this simple and practical guide towards achieving the latter. It is a distillation of some of the rich fruits of spiritual study.

Knowledge shared worldwide by the BKWSU offers a method for enabling all people to restore and accumulate within themselves a positive self-image. This then enables us to live with the love and respect towards others that must underpin any lasting peace.

Through developing different ways of thinking about ourselves, we can become better prepared for living in uncertain times.

Dadi Janki
Additional Administrative Head
Brahma Kumaris World Spiritual University

Contents

Leave worries aside and you will be surprised by the beauty of the sky and the colour of flowers, of the freshness of the breeze and the generosity of the sun. You will feel you are part of creation, and life will start to make sense. The greatest wealth is to appreciate what we have and what we are.

Life

Relationships

Thinking about others' actions can give you a headache. Think about what you have to do instead.

Do it and you will see how you then feel. No one can disturb your peace of mind. You are your friend or your enemy. Your limitations, weaknesses, expectations and negative habits threaten your peace and make you suffer.

Relationships

If someone is doing something wrong, instead of risking your peace by raising complaints in your mind, ask yourself "What can I do to benefit that person?"

Relationships

Good feelings for others are like ointments that heal wounds and re-establish friendship and relationships. Good feelings are generated in the mind, are transmitted through your attitude and are reflected in your eyes and smile.

Smiling opens the heart and a glance can make miracles happen.

Relationships

Humanity is like a tree. Each human being is connected with the Seed and belongs to the same tree. The beauty of the tree is that it has different branches and on each branch, numerous leaves.

All individuals are also different and have their own role. Think about what we have in common and you will appreciate every human being.

This is a key to remain at peace.

Relationships

One of the principal reasons for fear in our society is that we hear so much bad news about violence and conflict. Try changing the theme of your conversation and start talking about what life gives you.

It is necessary to create hope and enthusiasm for the future and to have a more positive view of the present reality.

In this way we promote peace.

Relationships

Cooperate with others.

Create cooperation.

Teach cooperation.

Inspire cooperation and you will find in your workplace a space to learn and a place for personal growth. Your motivation will shift from earning to learning.

Relationships

The root of suffering is attachment. You have created a space in your mind that holds a person or object as part of you. When that person or object is criticized, neglected or not with you, you feel pain in your mind and you experience a sense of loss.

If you want to be happy, you must learn to love and appreciate while remaining independent.

Relationships

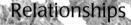

A sensible person knows that it is a waste of time and energy to get angry. Effort will then have to be made to reconstruct that relationship. It is much more useful to breathe deeply, pay attention to your attitude and answer without rushing.

In this way, improve and strengthen your relationships with others. Create trust and your mistakes will be forgiven.

Relationships

In order to create good relationships ...

- with your mind, think about what you have to learn from others,
- with your eyes, look into the good qualities of others,
- with your words, recognise, value and appreciate their accomplishments,
- with your actions, cooperate and do something for others.

Relationships

In order to live in peace, try not to depend on anyone and at the same time try to help others not to depend on you. Help them become independent, free and responsible for their lives. In the same way, ensure you do not cause anyone sorrow, and do not allow others to be a source of hurt for you.

Relationships

The most effective way to help others is always to remain peaceful. Be the example others want to see.

It is important to understand situations. They give you perspective. Apply what you understand because that gives you experience.

Relationships

If you think you can do something alone, either because you don't trust others to do it or because you feel you are the most qualified ...

- you will always be busy doing everything,
- you will be unhappy with others because they are not doing what you want,
- you will be dissatisfied. *mainly.*

It is more effective to invest your time in training and developing others. There is greater success in cooperation.

Relationships

Your words might impress others. People will say "He is a good speaker. What interesting things he said." But if you do not put into practice what you say, others will not feel inspired to do it. It is your actions which will inspire and show them how to do it.

ไม่รู้จัก

Relationships

28

When you make a mistake, learn from it, resolve not to repeat it and then forget about it. You will feel better again. Do the same with others. Instead of making their mistakes bigger, dissolve them in your mind and help them to also to forget about them.

(A sensible person does not criticise the mistakes of others. Instead, he learns from them for the future.)

Relationships

Tʜe great enemy of peace is ~~ego~~. *injustice* Ego makes you judge others and think about them in an unkind way. It makes you force others to do what you want. In this way you forget you are a student and that you are here to learn. *and so are THEY.*

Instead of learning, if you start giving advice, telling people what they should do and trying to change them, you are forgetting an important lesson in life. You can only change yourself, not others. *unless you really believe in yourself and believe in God's guidance*

Relationships

Give happiness and you will receive happiness.

Give peace and you will feel peaceful.

Give sorrow and you will get sorrow in return.

Create thoughts and words that give only peace and happiness. The world is filled with worry and sorrow. Do something different.

IMPORTANT LESSON IN LIFE

Relationships

In order to work peacefully within a group do the following. Give your idea as an expert, with authority and enthusiasm, then let go of it, but listen carefully and with interest to the ideas of others.

Love is shown through respect. When you respect, you can speak up clearly and the rest will listen to you. (TELL CHARLES) children copy their FATHER.

Relationships

Who are the thieves of peace ?

Why is peace lost in relationships ?

So right

Complaints, guilt and comparisons are the main destroyers of peace. Instead of complaining, share newness. Instead of looking for someone to blame, take responsibility for improving the situation. Instead of comparing yourself to others, value the good that is in them.

Relationships

Values

35

Values are related to each other as if they were members of a great family. From peace and happiness emerges inner joy. From this state of wholeness love awakens and with it the desire to share and give. Two of its relatives are tolerance and respect.

All values have a shared origin which unites them - the peace of spirituality. When you lose peace you begin to lose everything.

Values

When at peace you listen with attention and are totally present. This is an act of love that others appreciate. Love emerges from peace and manifests itself in the form of respect and acceptance.

Love is not only a feeling, but is expressed in words and actions.

Values

Love is the strength that gives you life. When you receive love you lose fear and you can give the best in you. The practical form of love is respect. Respect means acceptance of the fact that we are all different and unique and, at the same time, we all have something important and valuable to share.

Values

A mother teaches her child with love and patience until the child learns. Be a mother and teach your mind to have positive thoughts and to let go of worries. Then when your mind needs peace, it will obey you.

Values

Many believe that happiness is achieved through material wealth. It is true that it gives a temporary sense of well-being. A rich person is not someone who has more but someone who desires less.

Happiness is the result of total appreciation of all that life gives you at every moment.

Values

Learn to read reality with different eyes and you will have learnt the art of remaining peaceful and happy. When you see problems, you feel fear and tension. When you see problems as teachers you learn the lesson, become mature and grow strong.

Values

Happiness is the fruit of wealth. But of what wealth? Often, material wealth brings with it the fear of losing it. True wealth is knowledge that enables you to live life as the expression of your inner values.

Happiness grows when you do something for yourself and for others.

Values

You become whatever you think about deeply. Think only about peace, love and happiness. Feel those values as part of your life and you will become them.

Values

43

Our society encourages distraction and evasion as a means to experience happiness. But actually this takes you far away from yourself and just postpones dissatisfaction.

The true solution is to concentrate on what nourishes the spirit and gives you life.

Values

To love simple things is humility. It means to respect all that life presents to you. It means to appreciate and value everything appropriately. It means to remain focussed on your inner peace and not to lose your sense of personal well-being.

Values

To make good use of what you have and to let go of what you do not use is to live in a simple way.

Simplicity is to find beauty in the natural things in life and not be impressed by show.

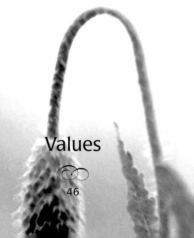

Values

46

D*etermination* is the *True* strength that will enable you to pass the barrier of useless thoughts in order to create positive thoughts and to be successful in whatever you wish. It comes from within and its partner is patience.

Patience teaches you not to push but rather to wait and appreciate the game of life instead, knowing that nothing remains the same, and everything will change at some point.

Values

Your internal dialogue establishes your way of seeing the world. When you make demands on and reproach yourself, you create a world of stress and pain. To be peaceful, create a loving dialogue with yourself, enabling your inner values to awaken and be expressed regardless of your external world.

Values

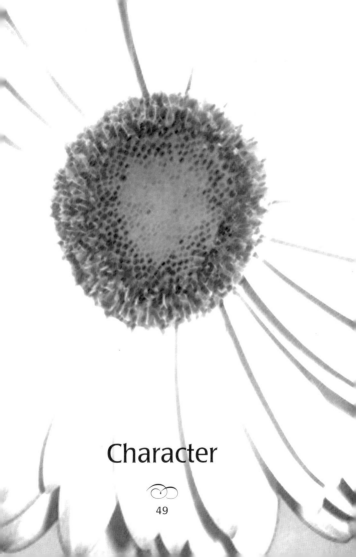

Character

49

To be peaceful you have to see yourself as a peaceful being. It means to think about being peaceful. It means that you have to be able to describe it in words. You must be capable of experiencing the feelings you would have if you reached that peaceful state.

Now believe in it.

If you feel it, it's real.

Simply work on it and keep it uppermost in your mind. Make it yours and it will become your natural behaviour.

Character

Say there is a weak spot, something you do not see or that you do not want to see about your character. The way to discover it is through others. They are the mirrors that reflect your personality. If something bothers you about someone, you are recognising an attitude that is actually within you. When you feel it does not affect you and you can respond calmly, it means that this weakness is no longer in you.

Character

When you do not upset yourself thinking about how others must change and instead you concentrate on your own change, good things start to happen. First, you will feel better about yourself. Second, you will start to have positive feelings towards others and start to understand them. Third, others start having a more positive attitude towards you.

There are many hidden benefits in personal change.

Character

Your attitude creates an atmosphere around you. Your attitude is the result of the way you feel and think. You communicate your attitude. Create a positive attitude, filled with good feelings, and even just your presence will do wonders in situations.

Character

Peace is not a passive attitude; it is an active state. It requires having constant attention and determination, in order to live and to respond as a peaceful being to any upset in life.

You need to be brave and vigilant.

Character

Anything you keep within you will automatically reveal itself. Therefore make sure you are always full of attainments in your character. These will be revealed through your eyes, your words and your behaviour and you will be capable of having great influence on others.

Character

The most powerful form of teaching is
by example.

What you see through your eyes creates great
impact. The heart accepts it and it does not
need many words.

You cannot impose peace through force but
you can be peaceful and create a
peaceful environment.

Character

To forgive and forget is to reflect love. Many are slaves of the past. Situations pass, they cease to exist, but they continue to be alive in the mind. Open your heart and be generous, free yourself from that sorrow, forgive and forget and you will live every moment in peace.

Character

To stay happy in every situation remember what has helped you, what has made life worthwhile. Forget the old, the things of no value, and what has stolen your dreams . You grow and progress in life thanks to what motivates and inspires you. You get depressed through remembering your weaknesses and mistakes.

Character

Worries are an illusion. They make you live in the future with the belief that you are busy and take you away from the present. Worries are an excuse for not doing what you really have to be doing.

A reactive person appears very busy and worried. With worry, no problems can be resolved.

A proactive person focuses attention on the present, acts with initiative, and the understanding that being calm and free from worry is far more effective.

Character

Your actions are the mirror of your thoughts. You can hide your thoughts but you cannot hide your actions. Have elevated thoughts and your actions will be elevated.

Character

Firm faith and self-confidence in your goals determine your destiny. Be sure not to forget your goals; do not allow doubts to come. Instead of seeing problems, see only opportunities.

Character

Self-control is not about suppressing emotions or tolerating the pressure of circumstances. Self-control is to be the creator of your thoughts and feelings, to be creative and find new answers. This·helps you to remain calm and cool.

Character

You search for something you know exists because you have experienced it in the past. All your searching ends when you find yourself. You do not need to go anywhere, or to look beyond yourself. Just become what you were before.

You fill your life with peace when you discover you only have to be yourself, to be what you have always been - a peaceful being.

Character

Secrets

To be peaceful is to be free from expectations and to want nothing from anyone. Take the initiative and be generous. Lead the way and do something. This is the secret to being content in all circumstances.

Secrets

Your peace will awaken the natural peace in others and will bring them hope.

You only believe in peace when you see it, that is, when you experience it. Concentrate on the centre of your forehead, sit behind your eyes and watch. That is where you create your thoughts. Teach your mind to reflect on peace.

Secrets

It is easy to create new things, change places or do something different. To keep that sense of newness that creates enthusiasm is more difficult. The secret of newness in life is not to do new things constantly, but to see everything you do with new eyes, new insights and a new perspective.

Secrets

Desires cause peace to disappear. You think that acquiring things will make you feel secure, but the reality is that the more you have the more fear there usually is of losing it, and the further you are from peace. Desires are the cause of all conflicts. When you want something and cannot get it you become frustrated. Learning to be free from desires is learning how to stay peaceful.

Secrets

Peace ends when you are emotionally involved in a situation. The practice of being an independent observer helps you stay stable and calm. It is the best way to approach a decision in any circumstance.

IT is also called
Selfishness -
To protect self.

Secrets

To attain peace when something unfortunate happens, open up to the possibility that there may be advantages hidden in that situation. Accept and learn, then your feelings will be positive and you will find solutions. You will have transformed a defeat into victory.

ITS also called caring

Secrets

Your true enemies - which destroy your peace - are negative habits. Your true attainment is the conquest of the self.

Secrets

Anger is also an enemy of peace. Anger comes as a result of an unfulfilled desire. Change the words "I want this, I want that" to "I am happy with what I have." To free yourself from "I want, I want" is to cease making withdrawals from your peace account.

Secrets

Why do you like sunsets so much ? Because
they take you beyond your physical
dimension. You experience peace and silence.
You sense that time stops, and you understand
what eternity means. It awakens your
dormant spirituality.

IT CAN ALSO AWAKENS YOUR
FEARS. We feel more alone

Whenever you have the chance, sit in front of
a sunset and relax. Do not analyse. Only watch
and observe and let profound feelings
of peace emerge.

Secrets

You do not lose peace because of circumstances but because of the struggle you create in your mind between what you think should be and what really is. " LIFE

To be accepting is not about being passive. It is to be aware of reality and to start working from there. quick WAY TO LoSE PEACE

Secrets

Your intellect follows your sight. Your mind runs behind. Teach your eyes to have an elevated vision and your mind will be relaxed.

Secrets

You spend most of your life running after things, doing things. You forgot that being comes before doing. Those who remember this secret make an effort to "be" and discover that when they stop and observe, life helps and brings whatever is needed.

Learning to be is learning to be at peace. It is our most fundamental nature. A TRUE SECRET.

Secrets

In a state of peace you can see that behind anger there is pain and sadness, that behind passive silence there could be fear. With mercy and acceptance you can respond to those situations.

Secrets

Self-consciousness distinguishes you from other animals. It enables you to be aware of your thoughts, feelings and emotions and to understand how they influence your behaviour. When your consciousness awakens, you start being truly free because you decide your destiny and take responsibility for your choices.

That's me.

Secrets

The best solutions to problems will not be the result of hard thinking. Use your time better by creating peaceful thoughts, and problems will cease to affect you. Do not try to solve everything on your own. Leave some space for God to come and help you.

Secrets

Silence

(Learn to create silence in your mind and peace will flourish in your soul. You will see life with other eyes. You will discover God's language. To be internally silent do not think too much. Trust yourself. Trust others. Trust life. You will find it is easier than it seems.)

TRUST GOD.
THE LORD SUSTAIN
MY SOUL.

Silence

Many times with the good intention of solving a problem you become part of the problem. In order to accept the problem it is more practical firstly to remain silent and serene. It is not necessary to understand the causes but to find solutions. Observe and reflect in silence and then make a decision.

GOOD ADVICE TO FAMILY AND REAL FRIENDS

Silence

In the ocean of silence you may discover your eternal treasures of peace, love and happiness. In silence, you can let bad feelings and past sorrows dissolve. In silence you can hear the whisper of God saying "Come child and rest with Me. You are a peaceful soul."

Silence

It is said that rest is best. Imagine an ocean of peace and silence and plunge into it. Let your mind relax and enjoy moments of tranquillity. Free yourself from wasteful thoughts. This is the best type of rest.

Silence

Silence calms your heart. It is a balm that heals the wounds of the soul. It strengthens the spirit and takes you to a world without sound where peace reigns.

Silence

Exercises

As you awaken, the first thought is your foundation for the rest of the day. When you open your eyes, sit for a moment and appreciate the gift of a new day, create a peaceful thought and enjoy some moments of silence.

Exercises

Develop the habit of getting up early and sitting in silence. Read a peaceful thought and reflect on it. Write down some ideas about this thought. Return to silence, allowing these ideas to take root inside you. Share your ideas with a person close to you. This practice will help you accept and cope with conflicts and difficult situations. It will help you stay happy and peaceful for the rest of the day.

Exercises

Peace is simplicity. Simplicity is beauty. Choose a day as your day of simplicity. Speak little, and listen with attention. Do something incognito and nice for a person you are close to. Eat simple and natural food. Create time periods for not doing anything - just walk, look around, live the moment. Have your mind open to a more profound and silent sensitivity. Appreciate each scene and each person as they are. In the evening, write down your discoveries. Observe the state of your mind.

Exercises

Think about all the things that worry you. Write them down on a piece of paper. Reflect on the ones you can control and write these on another piece of paper. Against each of the things you can control write what you could do about them. Free yourself from all the other worries which you cannot do anything about.

This is a good lesson on how to stay peaceful.

Exercises

Do this simple exercise for one minute each hour and you will be amazed at the result. Breathe slowly and deeply, relax and think ...

I am a peaceful being.

I am peaceful.

I love peace…

and I share peace with others.

Exercises

Do something altruistic for someone every day. Develop the habit of enjoying doing this, not for any reward but just for the sake of it and discover the fruit of that action.

The best gift is to give happiness and to finish sorrow.

Exercises

You are what you think. Think that you are a being of peace, and peace will become your new personality. Share good news with others. Always have something interesting prepared to share with those you meet. Remember to have a peaceful thought at least once a day.

Exercises

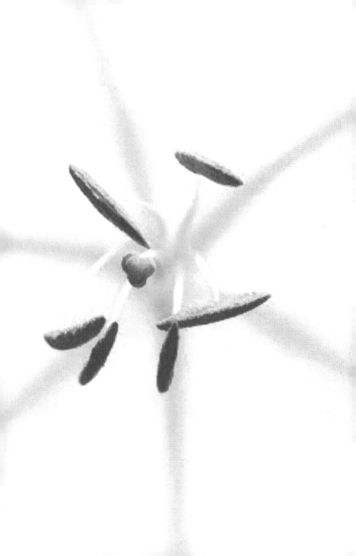

Brahma Kumaris World Spiritual University

The Brahma Kumaris World Spiritual University is an international organisation working at all levels of society for positive change. Established in 1937, the University now has over 8,500 branches in over 100 countries. It participates in a wide range of educational programmes in areas such as youth, women, men, environment, peace, values, social development, education, health and human rights.

In 1996, the University's Academy for a better World was opened in Mount Abu, India. The Academy offers individuals from all walks of life opportunities for life-long innovative learning. Residential programmes are centred on human, moral and spiritual values and principles. The University also supports the Global Hospital and Research Centre in Mount Abu, India.

Local centres around the world provide courses and lectures in meditation and positive values, supporting individuals in recognising their own inherent qualities and abilities and making the most of their lives.

All courses and activities are offered free of charge.

www.bkwsu.org

BRAHMA KUMARIS WORLD SPIRITUAL UNIVERSITY

WORLD HEADQUARTERS
PO Box No 2, Mount Abu 307501, RAJASTHAN, INDIA
Tel: (+91) 2974 - 238261 to 68 · Fax: (+91) 2974 - 238952
E-mail: bkabu@bkindia.com

INTERNATIONAL CO-ORDINATING OFFICE & REGIONAL OFFICE FOR EUROPE AND THE MIDDLE EAST
Global Co-operation House, 65-69 Pound Lane, London, NW10 2HH, UK
Tel: (+44) 208 727 3350 · Fax: (+44) 208 727 3351
E-mail:london@bkwsu.org

REGIONAL OFFICES

AFRICA
Global Museum for a Better World, Maua Close, Off Parklands Road, Westlands,
PO Box 123,Sarit Centre, Nairobi, Kenya
Tel: (+254) 20-374 3572 · Fax: (+254) 20-374 3885
E-mail: nairobi@bkwsu.org

AUSTRALIA AND SOUTH EAST ASIA
78 Alt Street, Ashfield, Sydney, NSW 2131, Australia
Tel: (+61) 2 9716 7066 · Fax: (+61) 2 9716 7795
E-mail:ashfield@au.bkwsu.org

THE AMERICAS AND THE CARIBBEAN
Global Harmony House, 46 S. Middle Neck Road
Great Neck, NY 11021, USA
Tel: (+1) 516 773 0971 · Fax: (+1) 516 773 0976
E-mail: newyork@bkwsu.org

RUSSIA, CIS AND THE BALTIC COUNTRIES
 2 Gospitalnaya Ploschad, build. 1, Moscow - 111020, Russia
Tel: (+7) 495 263 02 47 · Fax: (+7) 495 261 32 24
E-mail: moscow@bkwsu.org

www.bkwsu.org

Brahma Kumaris Publications
www.bkpublications.com
enquiries@bkpublications.com